MW01628603

hip dips

hip dips

STYLISH HOMEMADE DIPS TO WOW YOUR FRIENDS WITH

Love Food ® is an imprint of Parragon Books Ltd

Parragon
Queen Street House
4 Queen Street
Bath BA1 1HE, UK

Introduction and additional recipes by Lorraine Turner
Edited by Fiona Biggs
Designed by Emily Lewis and Sian Williams
Photography by Mike Cooper
Food Styling by Lincoln Jefferson

ISBN 978-1-4075-2618-8

Printed in China

NOTES FOR THE READER

This book uses imperial, metric, and US cup measurements. Follow the same units of measurement throughout; do not mix metric and imperial. All spoon measurements are level, unless otherwise stated: teaspoons are assumed to be 5 ml and tablespoons are assumed to be 15 ml. Unless otherwise stated, milk is assumed to be semi-skimmed, eggs and individual vegetables such as potatoes are medium, and pepper is freshly ground black pepper. People with liver disease and those with weakened immune systems should never eat raw fish. Recipes using raw or very lightly cooked eggs should be avoided by infants, the elderly, pregnant women, convalescents, and anyone with a chronic condition. The times given are an approximate guide only. Preparation times differ according to the techniques used by different people and the cooking times may also vary from those given. Optional ingredients, variations, or serving suggestions have not been included in the calculations.

contents

introduction

There is nothing like a selection of dips to add color and variety to the simplest of meals. The combinations of ingredients and flavorings are endless, and in addition to following the recipes here you can have fun experimenting with your own ideas.

If you are a novice in the kitchen, you will find that dips are one of the easiest things you can make, and will be appreciated by everyone who tries them. They need very little preparation, and often little or no cooking either. Even dips that require some cooking are often very simple and quick, so you can be confident of creating that perfect dip every time. You can also make them in advance so that you can sit down with your guests and enjoy a relaxed conversation instead of missing the fun because you are slaving away in the kitchen. In fact, making dips in advance often helps the flavors to develop.

The versatility of these tasty creations makes them very popular for a wide variety of occasions. Why not serve them with a selection of dippers on a party buffet table, for example, or pass them around in small individual bowls at a barbecue? They make great picnic and lunch bag fare too.

Dips also make irresistible appetizers for informal entertaining. Sharing a bowl of your favorite dip with other diners around a table is a great way to break the ice. For an even more informal atmosphere, why not arrange individual bowls of dips about the room for your guests to enjoy while they are wandering about?

The fact that dips are very quick to make is a definite plus if you are pressed for time. With today's increasingly busy lifestyles, dips offer an ideal way for the busy cook to save time in the kitchen. They also make satisfying snacks if you have no time to stop for a proper meal.

Ideal for entertaining

Dips will really come into their own if you suddenly find you have to entertain unexpected guests. It is amazing how easy it is to throw together a few tasty items from your pantry and refrigerator. For example, simply mix together a small jar of olives or sun-dried tomatoes, some cheese, yogurt, and perhaps a sprinkling of chopped herbs, and you will find that you have whipped up a delicious dip in the minimum amount of time possible.

Dips can be very nutritious. For example, cheesy dips or dips made with beans are rich in protein, which is necessary for your body to grow strong muscles, bones, teeth, and blood. Dips made with tomatoes are high in lycopene, a potent antioxidant that helps to protect against cancer and strokes. It may also help to prevent premature aging of the skin and reduce the risk of exercise-induced asthma. Dips that contain shrimp are excellent sources of magnesium, a mineral that is essential for good bone growth.

If you are preparing dips for a dieter or for someone who needs to keep saturated fats to a minimum, it is very easy to create a collection of delicious lowfat dips that will be suitable for any occasion. Try substituting reduced-fat sour cream, cream, and cheese for the whole milk varieties, or focus more on dips that are based on tomatoes or beans.

If you are catering for a fussy eater, don't forget that dips are a great way to disguise healthy ingredients. If you're dealing with difficult eaters, such as willful toddlers or finicky adolescents, or people who prefer to "nibble and graze" on small snacks throughout the day instead of eating a full meal, a selection of nutritious, well-chosen dips can help to make up any potential shortfall in a healthy diet. Camouflage any ingredients they might not be too keen on by putting them in a food processor with the other dip ingredients, processing them to a paste, then cooking and/or serving in the usual way.

You can also be creative with the containers you use for your dips. Experiment with dishes and bowls of different shapes, sizes, and colors. Alternatively, you could go all out for a more stunning display and use hollowed-out vegetables, such as red and orange bell peppers, squashes, cucumbers, or tomatoes. If you are catering for a children's party, how about preparing several different-colored dips for a little variety? If you slice the tops off some red and yellow bell peppers, hollow them out, put the dips inside, and then replace the tops, the children will have fun lifting off the tops and finding what's inside.

You can also let your imagination run with your dippers. The dips in this book can be served with an enormous range of dippers. In addition to offering sticks of raw carrots and cucumber, cherry tomatoes, radishes, and blanched vegetables such as zucchini to your guests, why not treat them to corn chips or potato/vegetable chips, small sausages, strips of pita, herbed crostini, crunchy breadsticks, mouthwatering morsels of focaccia, or succulent potato wedges? Or what about cubes of ham, pepperoni, or other meat and poultry, pieces of tasty fish, fresh seafood such as shrimp, and freshly cooked ravioli, wontons, or white mushrooms speared on forks? You could also cut some of the dippers, such as bread and carrots, into fancy shapes to entertain children. Cubes of cake, marshmallows, and pieces of fruit are ideal for serving with the sweet dips.

You'll also need something for spearing the dippers. Plain toothpicks are very handy for this purpose. However, there's no reason why you cannot create a more impressive display. If you have a fondue set you could offer fondue forks to your guests, or you could buy some small, pretty forks especially for the purpose.

When you are serving a selection of dips, try to keep them interesting by varying the textures and flavors. Perhaps try offering one or two creamy dips alongside a couple of tomato-based ones, or present some vegetarian alternatives to dips containing meat, fish, or shellfish. The combinations are truly endless, especially when it comes to flavorings—herbs, spices, sauces such as Tabasco—the only limit is your imagination, so be adventurous and increase your repertoire by adding new creations from time to time.

cool classics

In this chapter you will find many much-loved favorites, from delicious Guacamole and Tzatzíki, to mouthwatering Taramasaláta and the irresistible Middle-Eastern Baba Ghanoush.

guacamole

serves 4

2 large, ripe avocados
juice of 1 lime, or to taste
2 tsp olive oil
½ onion, finely chopped
1 fresh green chile, such as poblano, seeded and finely chopped
1 garlic clove, crushed
¼ tsp ground cumin
1 tbsp chopped fresh cilantro, plus extra to garnish
salt and pepper

Cut the avocados in half lengthwise and twist the 2 halves in opposite directions to separate. Stab the pit with the point of a sharp knife and lift it out.

Peel, then roughly chop the avocado halves and place them in a nonmetallic bowl. Squeeze over the lime juice and add the oil.

Mash the avocados with a fork until they are the desired consistency—either chunky or smooth. Blend in the onion, chile, garlic, cumin, and chopped cilantro, then season with salt and pepper to taste.

Transfer to a serving dish and serve immediately to avoid discoloration, sprinkled with chopped cilantro.

tapenade

serves 4

3½ oz/100 g canned anchovy fillets
12 oz/350 g black olives, pitted and coarsely chopped
2 garlic cloves, coarsely chopped
2 tbsp capers in brine, drained and rinsed
1 tbsp Dijon mustard
3 tbsp extra virgin olive oil
2 tbsp lemon juice

Drain the anchovies, reserving the oil from the can. Coarsely chop the fish and place in a food processor. Add the reserved oil and all the remaining ingredients. Process to a smooth paste. Stop and scrape down the sides of the food processor if necessary.

Transfer the tapenade to a dish, cover with plastic wrap, and chill in the refrigerator until required. If you are not planning to use the tapenade until the following day (or even the one after), cover the surface with a layer of olive oil to prevent it from drying out.

taramasaláta

serves 6

8 oz/225 g smoked cod roe
1 small onion, quartered
1 cup fresh white breadcrumbs
1 large garlic clove, crushed
grated rind and juice of 1 large lemon
⅔ cup extra virgin olive oil
6 tbsp hot water
pepper
black olives and capers, to garnish

Remove the skin from the fish roe. Put the onion in a food processor and chop finely. Add the cod roe in small pieces and process until smooth. Add the breadcrumbs, garlic, lemon rind and juice, and mix well together.

With the machine running, very slowly pour in the oil. When all the oil has been added, blend in the water. Season with pepper.

Transfer the mixture to a serving bowl and chill in the refrigerator for at least 1 hour before serving. Serve garnished with olives and capers.

aïoli

tzatzíki

aïoli

serves 4

3 large garlic cloves, finely chopped
2 egg yolks
1 cup extra virgin olive oil
1 tbsp lemon juice
1 tbsp lime juice
1 tbsp Dijon mustard
1 tbsp chopped fresh tarragon
salt and pepper
fresh tarragon sprig, to garnish

Ensure that all the ingredients are at room temperature. Place the garlic and egg yolks in a food processor and process until well blended. With the motor running, pour in the oil a teaspoon at a time through the feeder tube until the mixture starts to thicken, then pour in the remaining oil in a thin stream until a thick mayonnaise forms.

Add the lemon juice, lime juice, mustard and tarragon and season with salt and pepper to taste. Blend until smooth, then transfer to a nonmetallic bowl. Garnish with a tarragon sprig.

Cover with plastic wrap and refrigerate until required.

tzatzíki

serves 4

1 small cucumber
1¼ cups Greek-style yogurt
1 large garlic clove, crushed
1 tbsp chopped fresh mint or dill
salt and pepper

Peel and coarsely grate the cucumber. Put in a strainer and squeeze out as much of the water as possible. Put the cucumber into a bowl.

Add the yogurt, garlic, and chopped mint (reserve a little as a garnish, if liked) to the cucumber and season with pepper. Mix well together and chill in the refrigerator for about 2 hours before serving.

To serve, stir the dip and transfer to a serving bowl. Sprinkle with salt and serve.

baba ghanoush

serves 6

2 large eggplants
1 garlic clove, chopped
2 tsp ground cumin
4 tbsp tahini
2 tbsp lemon juice
4 tbsp plain yogurt
2 tbsp chopped fresh cilantro, plus extra to garnish

Preheat the oven to 425°F/220°C. Prick the eggplant skins and place them on a baking sheet. Bake for 1 hour, or until very soft. Remove from the oven and set aside to cool.

Peel off and discard the eggplant skins. Coarsely chop the flesh and place it in a food processor. Add the garlic, cumin, tahini, lemon juice, yogurt, and cilantro and process until smooth and combined, scraping down the sides of the food processor as necessary.

Transfer to a serving dish, sprinkle with a little cilantro, and serve. If you are cooking ahead, cover the dish tightly with plastic wrap and store in the refrigerator until 30 minutes before serving.

cheese & chive dip

serves 4

1 cup soft cream cheese
1 cup sour cream
¼ cup cheddar cheese, finely crumbled
1 garlic clove, crushed
2 tbsp snipped fresh chives
salt and pepper

Put the cream cheese and sour cream into a large bowl and beat together well.

Add the cheddar cheese, garlic, and chives and stir until combined. Season with salt and pepper to taste.

Transfer to a serving bowl or individual bowls and serve.

mango chutney

onion dip

mango chutney

serves 4–6

1 large mango, about 14 oz/400 g, peeled, pitted, and finely chopped
2 tbsp lime juice
1 tbsp vegetable or peanut oil
2 shallots, finely chopped
1 garlic clove, finely chopped
2 fresh green chiles, seeded and finely sliced
1 tsp black mustard seeds
1 tsp coriander seeds
5 tbsp light brown sugar
5 tbsp white wine vinegar
1 tsp salt
pinch of ground ginger

Put the mango in a nonmetallic bowl with the lime juice and set aside.

Heat the oil in a large skillet over medium–high heat. Add the shallots and fry for 3 minutes. Add the garlic and chiles and stir for 2 minutes, or until the shallots are softened, but not browned. Add the mustard seeds and coriander seeds and stir. Add the mango to the pan with the sugar, vinegar, salt, and ground ginger and stir. Reduce the heat and simmer for 10 minutes until the liquid thickens and the mango is sticky.

Remove from the heat and let cool. Transfer to an airtight container, cover, and chill for 3 days before using.

onion dip

serves 4

1 cup sour cream
3 tbsp dried onion flakes
2 beef bouillon cubes, crumbled

Combine the ingredients in a small bowl and mix very well.

Cover with plastic wrap and refrigerate for at least 30 minutes.

Stir thoroughly before transferring to a serving dish.

red bell pepper dip

serves 6

2 red bell peppers, halved and seeded
2 garlic cloves
1 tbsp olive oil
1 tbsp lemon juice
½ cup fresh white breadcrumbs
salt and pepper

Place the bell pepper halves and garlic in a pan and add just enough water to cover. Bring to a boil, then reduce the heat, cover, and simmer gently for 10–15 minutes until soft and tender. Drain and set aside to cool.

Coarsely chop the bell pepper halves and garlic and place in a food processor with the olive oil and lemon juice. Process to a smooth paste.

Add the breadcrumbs and process briefly until just combined. Season with salt and pepper to taste. Transfer to a serving bowl, cover with plastic wrap, and chill in the refrigerator until required.

bacon & sour cream dip

serves 4–6

6 strips lean bacon, rinds removed, if necessary
1¼ cups sour cream
1 bunch scallions, finely chopped
4 tbsp snipped fresh chives

Preheat the broiler. Place the bacon on the broiler rack and broil until well cooked and crisp, turning over once. Transfer to crumpled paper towels to drain and let cool. Put the sour cream in a bowl with the scallions and chives. Finely chop the bacon and add it to the bowl and stir together. Transfer to a serving bowl, cover, and chill until required.

vegetable yogurt dip

serves 4

1 cup cream cheese

½ cup plain yogurt or sour cream

1 tbsp fresh parsley, finely chopped

1 tbsp fresh thyme, finely chopped

2 scallions, finely chopped

Beat the cream cheese in a large mixing bowl until it is soft and smooth.

Add the yogurt, herbs, and one scallion. Mix well, cover with plastic wrap, and refrigerate for at least 30 minutes.

Stir thoroughly before transferring to a serving dish.

full of beans!

Beans are nutritious and satisfying, and what better way to entertain vegetarians and meat-eaters alike than with a delicious bean dip?

hummus

serves 6

14 oz/400 g canned chickpeas, drained and rinsed
1 garlic clove, crushed to a paste with ¼ tsp salt
3–4 tbsp tahini
2–4 tbsp freshly squeezed lemon juice
¼ tsp ground cumin
extra virgin olive oil or water
salt
paprika and chopped fresh flat-leaf parsley, to garnish

Put all but 1 tablespoon of the chickpeas into a food processor. Add the garlic and process to a thick, coarse paste. Add 3 tablespoons of tahini and process again until blended. Add 2 tablespoons of lemon juice, the cumin, and salt to taste and process until creamy. Taste and add extra tahini and/or lemon juice, if desired. For a thinner dip, with the motor running, drizzle in oil or water until you reach the desired consistency.

To serve, transfer to a serving bowl, then use the back of a spoon to make an indentation in the center of the dip. Put the reserved chickpeas in the indentation and drizzle with oil. Sprinkle with paprika and chopped parsley to garnish.

black-eyed pea dip with cilantro

serves 4

15 oz/425 g canned black-eyed peas
1 garlic clove, crushed
2 tbsp mild olive oil
1 tbsp white wine vinegar
1 tbsp finely chopped fresh cilantro
salt and pepper

Drain the peas, rinse under cold running water, and drain again. Transfer to a food processor and add the garlic and olive oil. Process until smooth.

Transfer to a serving bowl and stir in the vinegar, then stir in the chopped cilantro. Season with salt and pepper to taste, and serve.

creamy lima bean dip

serves 4

15 oz/425 g canned lima beans
1 garlic clove, crushed
2 tbsp mild olive oil
1–2 tbsp freshly squeezed lemon juice
1 tbsp finely chopped fresh parsley
salt and pepper
2 tsp finely grated lemon rind, to garnish
crudités, to serve

Drain the beans, rinse under cold running water, and drain again. Transfer to a food processor and add the garlic and olive oil. Process until smooth.

Transfer to a serving bowl and stir in enough lemon juice to taste, then stir in the chopped parsley. Season with salt and pepper to taste.

Garnish with the grated lemon rind and serve with a selection of crudités.

garlicky fava bean dip

fresh mint & bean dip

garlicky fava bean dip

serves 4–6

9 oz/250 g cooked fava beans
2–3 garlic cloves, halved
1–2 tsp ground cumin
1 tsp ground coriander
3 tbsp olive oil
juice of ½ lemon
salt and pepper
paprika and dried thyme, to garnish

Whiz the beans with the garlic, cumin, and coriander in a food processor, adding a little water from time to time to prevent the mixture from becoming too stiff. Gradually blend in the oil and lemon juice to form a smooth paste. Season with salt and pepper to taste.

Transfer the dip to a serving bowl. Serve while still warm or at room temperature, garnished with a sprinkling of paprika and thyme.

fresh mint & bean dip

serves 12

12 oz/350 g fresh shelled fava beans
1 cup soft goat cheese
1 garlic clove, crushed
2 scallions, finely chopped
1 tbsp extra virgin olive oil, plus extra to serve
grated rind and juice of 1 lemon
½ oz/15 g fresh mint leaves
salt and pepper

Bring a pan of lightly salted water to a boil, add the beans, and cook for 8–10 minutes, until tender. Drain well and let cool. When the beans are cool enough to handle, slip off their skins and put the beans in a food processor.

Add the cheese, garlic, scallions, oil, lemon rind and juice, and mint leaves to the beans and process until well mixed. Season the dip with salt and pepper to taste. Turn into a bowl, cover, and chill in the refrigerator for at least 1 hour before serving.

buttered nut & lentil dip

serves 4

4 tbsp butter
1 small onion, chopped
½ cup red lentils
1¼ cups vegetable stock
½ cup blanched almonds
½ cup pine nuts
½ tsp ground coriander
½ tsp ground cumin
½ tsp grated fresh ginger
1 tsp chopped fresh cilantro
salt and pepper

Melt half the butter in a pan, add the onion, and fry over medium heat, stirring frequently, until it is golden brown in color.

Add the lentils and stock. Bring to a boil, then reduce the heat and simmer gently, uncovered, for about 25–30 minutes, until the lentils are tender. Drain well.

Melt the remaining butter in a small skillet. Add the almonds and pine nuts and fry them over low heat, stirring frequently, until golden brown. Remove the skillet from the heat.

Put the lentils, the almonds, and the pine nuts into a food processor, together with any butter remaining in the pan. Add the coriander, cumin, ginger, and cilantro. Process for about 15–20 seconds, until the mixture is smooth.

Season the dip with salt and pepper and serve.

spicy bean dip

serves 4

2 tbsp olive oil
1 medium onion, chopped
2 garlic cloves, chopped
1 small red chile, finely chopped (seeded first if you want to reduce the heat)
15 oz/425 g canned red kidney beans, drained and rinsed
2 large tomatoes, peeled and chopped
1 tbsp tomato paste
½ cup red wine
salt and pepper

Heat the oil in a large skillet or pan over medium heat. Add the onion, garlic, and chile and cook, stirring, for 1 minute.

Add the beans, chopped tomatoes, and tomato paste to the skillet and cook, stirring, for 2 minutes. Pour in the wine and bring to a boil, stirring continuously. Reduce the heat to low, season with salt and pepper, and simmer, uncovered, for 15 minutes.

Remove the skillet from the heat and let cool to room temperature. Transfer half the mixture to a food processor, process until smooth, then pour it into a large serving bowl. Stir in the other half of the bean mixture. Serve immediately, or cover with plastic wrap and chill until required.

three bean salsa

split pea dip

three bean salsa

serves 4

2 tbsp olive oil
2 shallots, finely chopped
1–3 garlic cloves, crushed
1 fresh red serrano chile, seeded and finely chopped
2 oz/55 g freshly cooked fava beans
2 oz/55 g freshly cooked green beans, coarsely chopped
3 tbsp canned red kidney beans, rinsed, drained and coarsely chopped
2 tomatoes, about 4 oz/115 g, coarsely chopped
2 tbsp canned pickled chiles, drained and finely chopped
1 tsp honey, or to taste
1 tbsp chopped fresh cilantro

Heat the oil in a small heavy-bottom pan, add the shallots, garlic, and fresh chile and gently sauté, stirring frequently, for 5 minutes. Add the cooked beans, kidney beans, tomatoes, pickled chiles, and honey. Heat over medium heat, stirring occasionally, for 5–8 minutes until thoroughly heated through. Stir in the cilantro and serve.

split pea dip

serves 4

9 oz/250 g yellow split peas, rinsed
1 small onion, roughly chopped
1 garlic clove, roughly chopped
⅓ cup cup extra virgin olive oil
1 tbsp chopped fresh oregano, plus extra for sprinkling
1 small onion, very finely chopped, for sprinkling
salt and pepper

Put the split peas in a pan and add the roughly chopped onion, the garlic, and plenty of cold water. Bring to a boil, then simmer for about 45 minutes, until very tender.

Drain the split peas, reserving a little cooking liquid, and put in a food processor. Add 5 tablespoons of the oil and process until smooth. If the mixture seems too dry, add enough of the reserved liquid to form a thick smooth paste. Add the oregano and season with salt and pepper.

Transfer the mixture to a serving bowl and sprinkle with chopped onion and oregano. Drizzle over the remaining oil. Serve warm or cold.

refried bean dip

serves 6

14 oz/400 g canned red kidney beans
1 bay leaf
3 tbsp olive oil
2 garlic cloves, crushed
1 onion, finely chopped
1 small red chile, chopped
2 tomatoes, peeled and chopped
1 cup grated cheddar cheese
3 drops Tabasco sauce, or to taste
salt and pepper

Drain half of the kidney beans and put them in a large pan with the bay leaf. Cover with water, bring to a boil, then boil rapidly for at least 10 minutes. Reduce the heat to low and simmer for an additional 1¼ hours. Remove from the heat, drain, and discard the bay leaf.

Heat the olive oil in a skillet over medium heat, add the garlic, onion, chile, and tomatoes and cook, stirring, for 2 minutes. Mash the kidney beans using a potato masher, and then add to the pan with the remaining whole kidney beans and stir to combine.

Stir in the cheese and the Tabasco sauce and continue to cook, stirring, for about 5 minutes, or until the cheese has melted through. Season with salt and pepper to taste. Remove from the heat and serve immediately.

cheese & bean dip

serves 8

1 lb 12 oz/800 g canned cranberry beans, rinsed and drained
12 oz/350 g ricotta cheese
2 garlic cloves, roughly chopped
4 tbsp lemon juice
½ cup butter, melted
3 tbsp chopped fresh flat-leaf parsley
sunflower oil, for oiling
fresh flat-leaf parsley sprigs
salt and pepper
lemon wedges, to garnish

Place the beans, cheese, garlic, lemon juice, and melted butter in a food processor and process to a smooth paste. Add the chopped parsley and salt and pepper to taste and process again briefly to mix.

Lightly oil a mixing bowl. Scrape the mixture into the bowl and smooth the surface. Cover with plastic wrap and chill in the refrigerator until set.

To serve, turn out the dip onto a serving dish and fill the center with parsley sprigs. Garnish with lemon wedges and serve.

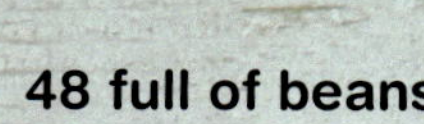

mint & cannellini bean dip

serves 6

6 oz/175 g canned cannellini beans, rinsed and drained
1 small garlic clove, crushed
1 bunch of scallions, roughly chopped
handful of fresh mint leaves
2 tbsp tahini
2 tbsp olive oil
1 tsp ground cumin
1 tsp ground coriander
lemon juice
salt and pepper

Put the beans into a bowl. Add the garlic, scallions, mint, tahini, and olive oil. Mash well until smooth.

Stir in the cumin, coriander, and lemon juice. Season with salt and pepper to taste. Mix thoroughly, cover with plastic wrap, and set aside in a cool place, but not the refrigerator, for 30 minutes to allow the flavors to develop fully.

Spoon the dip into individual bowls and serve at room temperature.

say cheese

What book on dips would be complete without a selection made from cheese? From feta cheese to cheddar cheese, and from goat cheese to cream cheese, these recipes will have you clamoring for more.

smoky cheese & bacon dip

serves 4

4 strips lean bacon

1 cup cream cheese

½ cup grated smoked firm cheese

1 cup sour cream

1 tsp wholegrain mustard

pepper

Preheat the broiler to medium. Arrange the bacon strips on the broiler pan, then transfer to the broiler and cook, turning once, for about 5 minutes or until the bacon is cooked through and crispy. Remove from the heat and let cool.

Meanwhile, put the cream cheese and smoked cheese into a large bowl and beat together well.

Add the sour cream and mustard and mix together thoroughly. Season with pepper to taste, then transfer to a serving bowl or individual serving bowls.

When the bacon is cool enough to handle, crumble the strips, stir half into the dip, sprinkle the remainder over, and serve.

herbed feta dip

serves 4–6

1 cup feta cheese, crumbled
¼ cup Greek-style yogurt
2 tbsp extra virgin olive oil
rind and juice of 1 small lemon
small bunch of fresh mint, chopped
small bunch of fresh flat-leaf parsley, chopped
½ red chile, seeded and chopped
pepper

Place the cheese, yogurt, and oil in a food processor and process for 30 seconds, until combined.

Scrape the mixture into a bowl and then add the lemon rind and juice, mint, parsley, and chile. Season with pepper to taste and mix well.

Place in the refrigerator to chill for 30 minutes before serving.

blue cheese dip with herbs

serves 4

1 cup soft cream cheese

1 cup sour cream

¾ cup firm blue cheese, very finely crumbled

1 scallion, white part only, very finely chopped

1 tbsp chopped fresh parsley

1 tbsp chopped fresh thyme

salt and pepper

Put the cream cheese and sour cream into a large bowl and beat together well.

Add the blue cheese, scallion, parsley, and thyme and stir until combined. Season with salt and pepper to taste.

Transfer to individual serving bowls and serve.

cheese & garlic dip

cheese & beer dip

cheese & garlic dip

serves 6

1 cup soft goat cheese
2 tbsp extra virgin olive oil, plus extra for oiling
2 tsp freshly squeezed lemon juice
2 garlic cloves, crushed
1 tsp hot or sweet smoked paprika
1 oz/25 g pitted green olives, finely chopped
1 tbsp chopped fresh flat-leaf parsley

Put the cheese in a food processor. With the motor running, add 1 tablespoon of the oil, drop by drop. Using a spatula, scrape down the sides of the bowl. With the motor running again, very slowly add the remaining oil and the lemon juice in a thin, steady stream. Add the garlic and paprika and process until well mixed.

Stir the olives and parsley into the dip. Turn the dip into a small serving bowl, cover, and chill in the refrigerator for at least 1 hour before serving.

cheese & beer dip

serves 6

3½ cups grated sharp cheddar cheese
1 small garlic clove, crushed
9 fl oz/250 ml beer
1 tsp powdered mustard
pinch of cayenne pepper
1 celery stalk, finely chopped
salt and pepper

Put the cheese, garlic, beer, mustard, and cayenne into a food processor and process. Taste and adjust the seasoning, then spoon into a bowl and stir in the celery. Cover and chill until required.

cheddar cheese dip with cranberries

serves 4

½ cup fresh whole cranberries
1 tbsp port (optional)
1 cup soft cream cheese
1 cup sour cream
½ cup sharp cheddar cheese, very finely crumbled
pepper

Put three quarters of the cranberries in a pan, add the port, if using, and cook over low heat for about 15 minutes.

Meanwhile, put the cream cheese and sour cream into a bowl and mix together well. Add the cheddar cheese and stir until combined.

Remove the cranberries from the heat and let cool to room temperature. Transfer to a food processor and process until smooth, then stir into the dip. Season with pepper to taste.

Transfer to a serving bowl or individual bowls and serve.

cheese & red wine dip

serves 4

1¾ cups very finely grated cheddar cheese
2 tbsp butter, softened
½ cup red wine
pepper

Put the cheese and butter into a bowl and mix together well.

Stir in the red wine and beat into the mixture until smooth. Season with pepper to taste.

Transfer to a serving bowl or individual bowls. Cover with plastic wrap and chill until required.

cheesy yogurt dip

cheese, garlic & herb dip

cheesy yogurt dip

serves 4

1 cup soft cream cheese
1 cup thick Greek-style yogurt
¼ cup finely grated sharp cheddar cheese
1 garlic clove, crushed
1 tsp wholegrain mustard
salt and pepper

Put the cream cheese and yogurt into a large bowl and beat together well.

Add the cheddar cheese, garlic, and mustard and stir until combined. Season with salt and pepper to taste.

Transfer to a serving bowl or individual bowls and serve.

cheese, garlic & herb dip

serves 4

1 tbsp butter
1 garlic clove, crushed
3 scallions, finely chopped
½ cup cream cheese
2 tbsp chopped fresh mixed herbs, such as parsley, chives, marjoram, oregano, and basil
ground paprika and fresh herb sprigs, to garnish

Melt the butter in a small skillet over low heat. Add the garlic and scallions and cook for 3–4 minutes, or until softened. Let cool.

Beat the cream cheese in a large mixing bowl until smooth, then add the garlic and scallions. Stir in the chopped herbs, mixing well.

Work the mixture together to form a stiff paste. Cover and chill in the refrigerator until ready to serve, garnished with the ground paprika and fresh herb sprigs.

rich double cheese dip

serves 4

2 cups grated cheddar cheese
½ cup cream cheese
1 garlic clove, crushed
2 scallions, white parts only, very finely chopped
1 tbsp wholegrain mustard

Preheat the oven to 350°F/180°C.

Put the cheddar cheese and the cream cheese in a mixing bowl and beat together. Stir in the garlic, scallions, and mustard.

Transfer to a ovenproof dish and cook in the preheated oven for about 15 minutes, until the cheese has melted through. Remove from the oven, transfer to a heatproof serving dish, and serve.

mediterranean cheese dip

serves 4

1 cup mascarpone cheese
1 cup Greek-style yogurt
½ cup finely grated Parmesan cheese
1 garlic clove, crushed
2 tbsp chopped fresh cilantro, plus extra to garnish
2 tsp lemon juice
12 black olives, pitted and very finely chopped
salt and pepper

Put the mascarpone cheese and yogurt into a bowl and beat together well.

Add the Parmesan cheese, garlic, chopped cilantro, and lemon juice and mix together. Stir in the chopped black olives and season with salt and pepper to taste.

Transfer the dip to a serving bowl or individual serving bowls, garnish with the chopped cilantro, and serve.

goat cheese dip with toasted almonds

serves 4

3 oz/85 g almonds
1 cup soft goat cheese
¼ cup plain yogurt
¼ cup mild olive oil
1 scallion, trimmed and very finely chopped
1 tbsp chopped fresh tarragon, plus extra to garnish
dash of Tabasco sauce
salt and pepper

Heat a dry skillet over medium heat, add the almonds, and cook, stirring continuously, for about 5 minutes, or until golden brown. Remove from the heat, transfer to a dish or plate, and let cool completely.

Put the cheese, yogurt, and olive oil into a food processor and process lightly until fairly smooth. Add the cooled almonds and process until smooth.

Transfer the mixture to a large serving bowl, add the chopped scallion, tarragon, and a dash of Tabasco sauce, then stir well. Season with salt and pepper to taste. Cover with plastic wrap and chill until required.

When ready to serve, garnish the dip with chopped tarragon.

hot stuff

This section presents a truly international array of hot and spicy dips, from Jamaica and the Caribbean to Mexico, and Turkey.

fiery bell pepper dip

serves 4

1 red bell pepper, skinned, seeded, and chopped
1 cup soft cream cheese
1 cup sour cream
1 garlic clove, crushed
½ red onion, very finely chopped
1 small red chile, seeded and very finely chopped
1 tbsp finely grated lime rind
salt and pepper

Put the bell pepper, cream cheese, and sour cream in a food processor and process until smooth. Add the garlic and onion and process again until smooth.

Transfer the mixture to a serving bowl or individual serving bowls and stir in the finely chopped chile and grated lime rind. Season with salt and pepper to taste and serve.

cream cheese & chile dip

serves 4

1 cup soft cream cheese
1 cup sour cream
2 scallions, white parts only, very finely chopped
1 small red chile, seeded and very finely chopped
1 tbsp snipped fresh chives
salt and pepper
large pinch of cayenne pepper, to garnish

Put the cream cheese and sour cream into a large bowl and beat together well.

Add the scallions, chile, and chives and stir until combined. Season with salt and pepper to taste.

Transfer to a serving bowl or individual bowls, garnish with a generous pinch of cayenne pepper, and serve.

roast tomato dip with spices

serves 4–6

6 vine-ripened tomatoes
1 red bell pepper, cut into quarters and seeded
1 garlic clove, unpeeled
1 red onion, cut into quarters
4 tbsp olive oil
1 small red chile, seeded and very finely chopped
1 tsp paprika (mild or hot, according to taste)
1 tbsp sherry
salt and pepper

Preheat the oven to 350°F/180°C.

Lay out the vegetables on a large baking tray, brush with olive oil, then roast in the oven, turning once halfway through cooking, for about 45 minutes, or until they are blistered and slightly charred.

Let cool. When cool enough to handle, peel the tomatoes and bell pepper, and squeeze the garlic from its skin. Transfer the tomato, bell pepper, garlic flesh, and onion to a food processor and process to a fairly smooth consistency.

Spoon the mixture into a large serving bowl and stir in the chile, paprika, and sherry. Season with salt and pepper to taste and serve.

caribbean salsa

jamaican salsa

caribbean salsa

serves 4–6

1 small ripe mango, peeled
1 small ripe papaya, peeled
1 fresh habanero chile
4 scallions, finely chopped
1–2 tsp maple syrup
½ small fresh coconut
1 tbsp chopped fresh cilantro
pepper

Remove and discard the mango pit. Finely chop the flesh and put in a bowl. Scoop out and discard the papaya seeds. Finely chop the flesh and add to the mango. Cut the chile in half, remove and discard the seeds and membrane, and finely chop. Add to the fruit with the scallions and maple syrup.

Discard any outer shell from the coconut, leaving the white flesh. Grate the coconut flesh. Add to the fruit with the cilantro and add pepper to taste. Spoon into a serving dish. Cover and let stand in a cool place, but not the refrigerator, for at least 30 minutes to allow the flavors to develop.

jamaican salsa

serves 4–6

1 large ripe banana
rind of 1 lime
2 tbsp freshly squeezed lime juice
2 oz/55 g drained canned corn
2 ripe guavas, peeled and pitted
1–2 fresh Jamaican hot chiles, seeded and finely chopped
1 small red onion, finely chopped
1 tsp honey, or to taste
1¼ cups plain yogurt
1 tbsp chopped fresh cilantro
pepper

Peel the banana and mash in a nonmetallic bowl. Add the lime rind and juice, then gently stir until the banana is thoroughly coated in the lime juice. Stir in the corn.

Add the guavas to the bowl with the chiles, onion, and honey.

Stir in the yogurt with the cilantro and add pepper to taste. Stir well, then spoon into a serving bowl. Cover and let stand in a cool place, but not the refrigerator, for at least 30 minutes to allow the flavors to develop.

spicy avocado dip

serves 4

2 large avocados
juice of 1–2 limes
2 large garlic cloves, crushed
1 tsp mild chile powder, or to taste

Cut the avocados in half. Remove the pits and skin and discard.

Put the avocado flesh in a food processor with the juice of 1 or 2 limes, according to taste. Add the garlic and the chile powder and process until smooth.

Transfer to a large serving bowl or individual serving bowls and serve.

tropical salsa

serves 4

1 small wedge watermelon, about 4 oz/115 g
2 blood oranges, or 1 red grapefruit
1–2 fresh green jalapeño chiles
2 tsp honey
2 oz/55 g preserved ginger, drained, with 2–3 tsp syrup from the jar reserved
1 tbsp chopped fresh mint

Peel and seed the watermelon and finely chop the flesh. Put in a bowl. Working over the bowl to catch the juices, peel the oranges, removing and discarding all the bitter white pith. Separate into segments, chop the flesh, and add to the watermelon.

Cut the chiles in half, remove and discard the seeds and membrane, and finely chop. Add to the fruit with the honey. Stir well.

Finely chop the ginger and add to the bowl with the ginger syrup. Add the mint and stir well. Transfer the salsa to a serving bowl. Lightly cover and let stand in a cool place, but not the refrigerator, for 30 minutes to allow the flavors to develop. Stir again and serve.

turkish salsa

tex-mex salsa

turkish salsa

serves 4

1–2 fresh red jalapeño chiles, halved, seeded and finely chopped
4 scallions, finely chopped
2 oranges
1 ripe pomegranate
2 ripe figs
2 tsp honey
1 tbsp snipped fresh chives
1 tsp toasted cumin seeds

Put the chiles in a bowl with the scallions. Working over the bowl to catch the juices, peel the oranges, removing all the white pith. Separate into segments, finely chop the flesh, and add to the chiles and scallions.

Cut the pomegranate in half and scoop out the seeds. Add the seeds to the orange mixture. Lightly rinse the figs and finely chop.

Add the chopped figs to the bowl with the honey and chives. Stir well and spoon into a nonmetallic serving dish. Cover and set aside in a cool place, but not the refrigerator, for 30 minutes to let the flavors develop. Sprinkle with the cumin seeds and serve.

tex-mex salsa

serves 4

1 large avocado
2 tbsp freshly squeezed lime juice
1 white onion, coarsely grated
1–3 fresh green jalapeño chiles
1–2 tsp maple syrup
2 oz/55 g canned pinto beans, rinsed and drained
8 oz/225 g ripe tomatoes, seeded and finely chopped
1 tbsp chopped fresh cilantro

Halve and pit the avocado. Peel, then finely chop the flesh. Put in a bowl, pour over the lime juice, and gently stir until the avocado is coated in the juice. Stir in the onion.

Cut the chiles in half and remove and discard the seeds and membrane. Finely chop the flesh. Add to the avocado with the maple syrup.

Coarsely chop the pinto beans and add to the bowl with the tomatoes and cilantro. Stir well, spoon into a nonmetallic serving dish, cover, and set aside in a cool place, but not the refrigerator, for 30 minutes to allow the flavors to develop.

mint & spinach chutney

serves 4–6

1 cup tender fresh spinach leaves
3 tbsp fresh mint leaves
2 tbsp chopped fresh cilantro leaves
1 small red onion, roughly chopped
1 small garlic clove, chopped
1 green chile, chopped (seeded, if liked)
2½ tsp granulated sugar
1 tbsp tamarind juice or juice of ½ lemon

Put all the ingredients in a food processor and process until smooth, adding only as much water as necessary to enable the blades to move.

Transfer to a serving bowl, cover, and chill in the refrigerator for at least 30 minutes before serving.

lowfat yogurt dip

serves 4–6

4 oz/115 g dried apricots
⅔ cup lowfat Greek-style yogurt
3 tbsp rolled oats
1–2 tsp honey, or to taste
1 fresh green jalapeño chile, seeded and finely chopped
6 scallions, finely chopped
1 carrot, about 4 oz/115 g, peeled and grated
2 tbsp chopped fresh mint
few dashes Tabasco, to taste
pepper

Finely chop the apricots and put in a small bowl. Add the yogurt with the rolled oats and honey.

Stir well, then add the chile, scallions, carrot, and mint. Season with pepper to taste. Stir again, then add the Tabasco sauce to taste.

Spoon into a serving bowl. Lightly cover and let stand in a cool place, but not the refrigerator, for at least 30 minutes to allow the flavors to develop. Store in the refrigerator if keeping for longer.

spicy shrimp dip

serves 4

3 tbsp olive oil
1 large garlic clove
1 small red chile, seeded and very finely chopped
14 oz/400 g raw shrimp, peeled and deveined
3 tbsp sour cream
juice of ½ lemon
1 tbsp finely chopped fresh flat-leaf parsley
thin strips of lemon rind, to garnish

Pour the olive oil into a skillet and warm over medium heat. Add the garlic and chile and cook, stirring continuously, for 1 minute. Add the shrimp and cook, stirring continuously, for another 3 minutes, or until the shrimp are cooked (but do not overcook).

Remove from the heat, transfer to a food processor, and pulse briefly until combined.

Transfer the mixture to a large serving bowl. Stir in the sour cream, lemon juice, and parsley, then garnish with thin strips of lemon rind. Serve immediately, or cover with plastic wrap and chill until required.